CLASS CLOWN

CLASS CLOWN

Poems

PINO COLUCCIO

BIBLIOASIS
WINDSOR, ONTARIO

FIRST EDITION

Library and Archives Canada Cataloguing in Publication

Coluccio, Pino, author
    Class clown : poems / Pino Coluccio.

Issued in print and electronic formats.
ISBN 978-1-77196-155-4 (softcover).--ISBN 978-1-77196-156-1 (ebook)

    I. Title.

PS8605.O493C53 2017   C811'.6   C2017-903645-9
                                                           C2017-903646-7

Edited by Zach Wells
Copy-edited by Emily Donaldson
Typeset by Chris Andrechek
Cover designed by Ellie Hastings

Published with the generous assistance of the Canada Council for the Arts, which last year invested $153 million to bring the arts to Canadians throughout the country and the financial support of the Government of Canada. Biblioasis also acknowledges the support of the Ontario Arts Council (OAC), an agency of the Government of Ontario, which last year funded 1,709 individual artists and 1,078 organizations in 204 communities across Ontario, for a total of $52.1 million, and the contribution of the Government of Ontario through the Ontario Book Publishing Tax Credit and the Ontario Media Development Corporation.

PRINTED AND BOUND IN CANADA

Contents

Thirsty and Miserable   11
The Office   12
The Incredible Shrinking Man   13
Old Man Feeding Ducks   14
Happiness   15
This is Bendale   16
Death of a Cover Band Guitarist   17
Unlikeable   18
City Sunsets   19
A Toronto Bike Courier Foresees His Death   20
Love and Sleep   21
Pretty in Pink   22
Entry Level   24
$ 25
The Chicken   26
The Random Rearranger   27
Father Tony   28
1932–2007   30
All That's Left   31
The Chandler   32
Canadians   33
Be a Man   34
At a Wedding   35
The Guy Not Taken   36
Supply Chain   37
The Model   38

The Apple   39
Feeding Frenzy   40
The Emperor's New Prose   41
Subdivisions   42
Class Clown   43
Planes, Trains and Automobiles   44
Groundhog Day   45
Hallmark   46
Casualties   47
The Stranger   48
Smile   49
Martial Arts   50
Old-timer   52
Beta   53
Poets   54
Judas   55
Manifesto   56
Bow Tie   57
Candles   60

For Rebecca, Bonnie, Gabrielle,
Lily, Alicia, Antonia and Sadie

So swallow all your tears my love
and put on your new face.
You can never win or lose
if you don't run the race.

–The Psychedelic Furs

Thirsty and Miserable

I will arise and ride now, my bike to the LCBO
and a can of lager buy there of malted barley made.
And fill a frosted mug with it and in its golden glow
lie alone with a bit less dread.

And I shall decompress then, by icy ale made warm,
and down a smoked meat sandwich and a second sweaty can.
How utterly the barley and the hops and yeast transform
the unassuming water and the man.

It's sketchy drinking solo but it is that which it is.
I heard all day and hear now at my local liquor store
pulled tabs pop on Stiegl cans and poured out tresses fizz.
I hear it in the dry throat's core.

The Office

1.

My days are like the invoices,
and here and there a letter,
that cross my desk at work en route
to the maw of the bottomless shredder.

2.

My job is like the copier
that copies what I feed it:
days and weeks, a life that changes
less the more I lead it.

3.

I feel like a staple.
The world isn't kind.
It's a Swingline and I'm so—
ka-thump—in a bind.

The Incredible Shrinking Man

At times I almost see it in her eyes.
My shrunkenness has cut me down to size.
My measurements appall her.
And every day I get a little smaller.

Our happy past in pictures on the walls—
they're like an accusation, all those smiles.
There's really no escape,
our destiny is magnitude, is shape.

It happens to us all I guess,
we have ourselves to thank.
We have such giant shoes to fill—
our own before we shrank.

Old Man Feeding Ducks

Ducks
gathered
for the crumbs
he tossed from shore.
Till one day no old man to toss them more.

Happiness

Happiness is fine,
from 12 to 29.
But thinning-haired and 30,
you crave the sure and sturdy.
You seek a house and wife
and benefits—a life,
built to your father's design,
that's safe to age and die in.

This is Bendale

Where nothing is old.
There's lots of payday loan shops
and shops that buy gold,
but no old churches
or an old bronze statue
and you can't look at masterpieces
looking back at you
in Bendale.

Where you're often alone,
flopped out on the couch
in the glow of your phone.
But where you gonna go to,
there isn't a square
where people hang out
and no fast metro there
in Bendale.

It isn't a place.
Or not a soft brick one
but one made of glass,
that doesn't show a self off
or have one to show,
but mirrors back the clouds
to the clouds as they blow
past Bendale.

Death of a Cover Band Guitarist

He'd learned on it and played it
in bars and always made it
do the talking for him.
He always had it near him.
And now it's gone as quiet,
with nobody to play it,
as he is, gone away,
with no guitar to play.

Unlikeable

Friends are the books of the illiterate.
Hey, you up for drinks?
Who has time for friends the bookish
thirty-something thinks.

But when he's pushing sixty,
and his nights, though numbered, seem endless,
who has time for books he'll groan.
Books are the friends of the friendless.

City Sunsets

They velvet-slipper their procession
with the cars that domino
their brake lights homeward after work,
over evening's purple snow.

They inch a never-ending arc
on hidden Forest Hill, its tawny
blondes who strut in Uggs and Lulus,
and a Filipino nanny.

They hear a roti shop's confession
and a billboard praising beer.
And lessen age and frailty's weight,
and calm a squabble, for a night.

City sunsets are the Pope
in his mantle doling hope
to dollar stores and sprinkling pity
on the rooftops of the city.

A Toronto Bike Courier
Foresees His Death

I know that I shall meet my end
between a tire and streetcar track.
The laws of motion never bend.
Wrists and femurs often crack.

I rent a basement near the ROM.
My neighbours are creative types.
They will not see me not glide home
or miss me in their coffee shops.

It's not the herb that makes me ride,
and plus, I have a PhD.
I just feel trapped when I'm inside.
The interwebs are not for me.

I tallied every big what if.
It was a quick and easy math
to pedal from a beta's life
towards an alpha's metal death.

Love and Sleep

We talk of both as something
we fall into
and aren't up for long
when we begin to
fall asleep and fall
in love again.
No one was around
when they began,
though sleep is older. Both
involve a bed.
And not enough of either
makes us sad.
Shallow and short, or long
and dreamy and deep:
these are the kinds of love
and the kinds of sleep.

Pretty in Pink

Maybe it's his granny glasses,
pompadour and hat,
a kid who thinks he's funny
when the world is laughing at

how weak he is, how hard he tries
to shake what he's afraid of:
a future without Andie,
the molecules he's made of.

A kid who doesn't drink and drive
because he rides a bike—
some boys women like as friends,
some boys women like.

Maybe it's because he isn't
Blane, who doesn't let
people stick a label on him.
Duckie doesn't get

that what makes Blane and Andie
a good match is that they're strong,
and feel a need to be themselves,
and not just to belong.

But really it's another why
that Duckie hankers after,
when he goes out riding in the rain.
Its edges are much softer.

It's not the clipboard causal kind
a lab can prove as true.
But why things *have to be* the way
they are. I wish I knew.

Entry Level

1.

20% of life turns out
80% of the joy
we cherish down its slope.
The rest is hanging on in nervous hope.

2.

When, not if, I wonder if
at last becomes if only,
I want to get out on my own
will turn into I'm lonely.

3.

Seeya later escalator.
In a while turnstile.

$

1.

He lay awake on his stomach
then flipped himself like a burger
and lay awake on his back,
blinking up at the black.

2.

The social lines are drawn
very early on:
you either join the lender class
or borrowed money spender class.

3.

They buy a bite of happiness
and spoon themselves a hole
right through the bottom of
consumerism's bowl

The Chicken

The weekend scuds,
Monday thuds,
bile and boredom thicken.
My days are feathers. Pluck me, Work,
pluck me. I'm a chicken.

The Random Rearranger

The Random Rearranger who hides the channel changer
helps some old fart find he's losing more of his mind
with each year that passes. And each time his glasses
vanish from their case, they're like his late wife's
face:
at times so real and near, only to disappear.
The missing cordless, keys and recent memories
remind him what's in store:
he's going to lose much more.

Father Tony

Look, it's Father Tony,
in the sun that's sinking down,
on the piazza, full of blessings
for our townsmen and our town.

For our town's little church
and our church's little tower,
and the tower's little bell
duly clanging out the hour,

and sometimes for the angelus'
low steady knell.
For the dusky patch of heaven
at the bottom of the well.

A blessing for the plumpy
peasant woman drawing water
in her kerchief and her apron,
and a blessing for her daughter,

and a blessing for the sun
when it's glarey, and the showers,
and the slim green snake
disappearing through the flowers.

For the ploughman's silhouette
against the sun about to sink
behind our town's surrounding hills,
and for the sky all gold and pink.

And one for the cantina
and the village drunkards there,
and the black cat that oversees
the empty village square.

And one for the cemetery's
cypresses and hawks,
and its shovel, and the sound it makes
rasping in the rocks.

Based on "Benedizione," *by Giovanni Pascoli*

1932–2007

Born in Campania.
Died in Ontario.
Never lived anywhere,
Uncle Saverio.

All That's Left

He won it at the fair,
a shiny plastic horn,
and toots it unreborn
hoofing slowly home;

a sound with something in it
of the candyfloss he had,
and the lights looking happy
and the clowns looking sad.

The storm that shook our little
city can be heard,
the thunder's every word,
in droplets off our roof.

The living match that was
a firefly revealed,
even as it died,
spring in every field.

Based on "La trombettina," *by Corrado Govoni*

The Chandler

The dipped-in-tallow tapers
Galileo lit
and cracked his head by on his books,
all Greek to me, at night—

it was me who dipped them,
who with my candle spark,
who kindled with my candles
science in the dark.

Canadians

Kowalczyk and Ferreira,
diverse and yet the same.
They killed themselves to come here,
then cursed the day they came.

Be a Man

1.

Curt had cats, Pumpkin and Sparky.
And Peppy and Sadie, two dogs.
We had pigeons and rabbits but sometimes we ate them.
Once in a while when I think of my parents,
I borderline hate them.

2.

We learn too late (*if* we learn)—
the ancient human curse—
that things in fact were way way better
back when they were worse.

3.

Life's favourite weather is mostly a storm
and the childhood my little mom knitted me,
the guilt and the worry of wanting me warm—
I wish it still fitted me.

At a Wedding

No drivel-dravel bound for the remainder bin I hope,
but a total, bracing classic all the centuries won't solve.
I hope your love is facing pages finishing a self.

The Guy Not Taken

I'll tell it with a twisted glee
when I've lost my hearing and my hair.
Two men diverged on the street, and she,
she followed after him, not me.
It was all downhill from there.

Supply Chain

She takes her place each morning
and she sews and sews and sews,
same as all the other girls
in rows and rows and rows,
girls like the stitches
in my clothes and clothes and clothes.

The Model

With guys who came and went, or with her dog,
or with her mom. Trying to look triumphant
pulling up in her new car. On beaches
in bikinis or in LBDs
in clubs, in all her pics on Facebook she looks
pretty much the same. The gowned and hatted
happy uni grad,
whose same smile or half-smile is always sad.

The Apple

His job, making screen doors,
was the biggest thing he hated,
and he wished the town he lived in
and his Taurus were cremated,
and his jeans and what he wanted once
and baseball cap were faded,
and he bitched but wouldn't quit or move away.

He knew if he had muscles
but he hated lifting weights,
or if his looks were good but anyways
he spent his Friday nights,
him and Luke, his one good buddy,
playing Doom, and ifs and mights
and bitches and all bonds were bonds to sorrow.

Soon the staff in burger joints
are kids who call you sir.
How did the days that wouldn't end
end up a life in such a blur?
And now you know what you've become
is what you really always were.
You played it safe and bit by bit it killed you.

Feeding Frenzy

Hipster chill meets über tony
at Baloney à la Carte,
where baloney is an art.
       All-organic green baloney
       that's sustainable and smart:
hipster chill meets über tony
at Baloney à la Carte.
       Mortadella seems so phony,
       this baloney's full of heart—
       load the grinder, let it start.
Hipster chill meets über tony
at Baloney à la Carte,
where baloney is an art.

The Emperor's New Prose

They lacked the nerve to tell him,
as he strutted through the square,
that his poetry was prose
and that his bum was really bare.

Afraid to seem simplistical,
they struck a learned pose
at the emperor's bare bum
and at his poetry, bare prose.

Subdivisions

Years so like a movie
that's left a hazy trace,
whose plot you don't remember,
whose mood you can't erase.

It's things you don't remember
that weigh on you the most.
Memories are corpses,
forgotten things, a ghost.

But what *do* I remember
(when I bother to that is)?
As much what didn't happen.
As much what never was.

My father's cigarette smoke
when I cracked the door ajar,
having kicked my way home after school,
that told me he was there.

Kind ears captive to the beers
you bought them but don't tell.
And the band played "Stairway to Heaven,"
and the band played "Highway to Hell."

Class Clown

They'd all be like, never say never
in classes we had, but whatever.
I turned to the windows and hallways
that always said always say always.

Planes, Trains and Automobiles

My sweater-vests and cardigans,
my necessary junk,
my shower-curtain rings of course:
my life is in my trunk.

A framed glossy picture
of Marie, my better half,
but not her perfume (jasmine),
her cooking, or her laugh.

From New York to Chicago
and Chicago to New York,
the days are seldom sunny,
the nights are always dark.

Pretty soon I'll have to pack it in,
I'm getting old.
There's not a lot worth having
that a travel trunk can hold.

Groundhog Day

It's yesterday again.
I almost don't remember
when I woke up in the morning
and yesterday was gone.

I almost don't remember
when the day I'd gotten wrong
was yesterday and gone,
cancelled with an x.

The day I'd gotten wrong
didn't really matter,
it was cancelled with an x.
There used to be tomorrow.

It doesn't really matter
when I wake up in the morning.
There used to be tomorrow
but it's yesterday again.

Hallmark

Today you're 52.
My birthday wish for you
is all the dreams and drive
you had at 25.

Casualties

Bygone women of the 80s,
still allowed to look like ladies,
the way you had of showing sweetly
by hiding things, but not completely,
never not with nylons on—
how I hate it that you're gone.
Replaced, in all the malls, by teens
who slump along in Uggs and jeans
and yoga pants. It leaves me cold.
I'm much too young to be this old.

The Stranger

At work he avoided the lunchroom—
he hated the klatches of staff—
and ate his panino outside on a bench.

On weekends he tried hard to laugh,
and tried hard to hide he was trying,
and got home tired from trying so hard,
but never believed he was lying.

And gawked, with friends, when they did,
at waitresses he hated.

They all said, after it happened,
their first green grapple with death,
he was someone they'd all been around for years
who'd been around them but not with.

Smile

Impossible to fake,
synonymous with everything's OK,
smiles are why I flinch when aimed phones take (*Say
cheese!*)
my picture, and swerve the other way.

Other people's faces overflow,
heads on beers their effervescent grins.
Mine's a nervous effort not to show
what's missing from my heart, a mannequin's.

A model's beamy eyes
and smile advertise
feeling more accomplished, less alone—
a life that's so much better than my own.

But even as it gathers in the years,
I tell the camera pictures are like stars:
tiny points of light
against a huge night.

Martial Arts

1.

He sees her, he sees her, and ribbit he says,
and ribbit again from his log.
She thinks he's gross and leaves him there.
He dies a horrid frog.

2.

What are all excuses but
a case of seeing double:
what you ought to do, and how
to spare yourself the trouble.

3.

She isn't one for debts and duties,
sentiments or high ideals.
Life is full of needs and beauties,
what she wants and how she feels.

4.

Sure, no problem, really,
don't be sorry, friendship's fine.
She offers him some water. Thank you.
Water and not wine.

5.

You don't believe in happy endings do you?
I sure don't, not even just a little.
How's it happy getting old and dying?
You're happy, if you're happy, in the middle.

Old-timer

No trace of him on Facebook
or anywhere online,
but burping demijohns of must
on plinths for making wine.

You see by what he did
the main of what his leanings were:
the pigeon coop he made
from hockey sticks and chicken wire.

Born before the atoms vs.
bits and bytes divide,
he knew or thought he knew
his proper side.

Beta

The king of smarm,
a total worm,
he makes his fish-eyes
and they squirm.

The clammy grip
that seems to plead.
They like desire
in men, not need.

It's not not getting
lucky he's
afraid of, but
epiphanies

of being second
rate, and so
he goes for girls
he knows by now

he'll never get.
That's him there,
with the wine glass
full of beer.

Poets

How unmalformed their minds are,
how lofty and unlewd—
no time for sex or TV,
no time for rock or food.

What singleness of heart—they only
love the written word.
And how much time and money they have,
how sure they should be heard.

Judas

A shame if he went easy on the sugar.
The Lord's steak was, I hope, big but not bigger
than Judas'. I hope he didn't think
how much the wine would cost and just got drunk.
For unlike Jesus, Judas never knew
that this would be his own last supper too.

Manifesto

The violinist
or the fiddler—
who's the greater,
who's the littler?

Glug a brew
or sip a vino—
not a poet
but a Pino.

Bow Tie

It's midnight and the scooters
and the footsteps die away,
and the voices and the neon
OPEN sign in a cafe.

The stars are like the bubbles
in a glass of rum and Coke
and a thick hush hangs
over everything like smoke.

The river's got a secret
it's excited not to keep,
and when the last crickets
in the bushes are asleep,

he ambles by
in a black bow tie.

Looking slicker than a pistol
with a walking stick of crystal,
and a rose as red as hell
bleeding out of his lapel,

he says hello.
I watch him go.

Good night, good night, good night, he says,
buona notte.

To the tumbler full of stars
and the shuttered divey bars.
And he tips his tall top hat
to a softly stalking cat.

...

The sky at night, a sleek
black cat, when it's dawn,
becomes the cat's mouth
in a long pink yawn.

The moon's shift is over
and the streetlights flicker off
and you hear somebody start his car
and hear somebody cough.

Windows open up like eyes
onto the river down below,
in the amber light of morning,
in the amber morning's glow,

and floating by,
a black bow tie.

And the river rocks it gently
and it bobs along contently,
followed slowly as it goes
by a top hat and a rose—

he says hello.
I watch him go.

Good night, good night, good night, he says,
buona notte.

To a happy past and sad,
and to one I never had.
And the skyline and the sky
and to everything, good bye.

Based on "Vecchio Frack," *by Domenico Modugno*

Candles

They grace both cakes and churches.
We dig for them in drawers when power fails us.
The clean slow burn of mixing wax and wicks.

The dipped-in-tallow taper
of the Roman on his road,
or beeswax model Benedictines read by.
The paraffin that's honeysuckle-scented.
The chunky pillar, jelly jar,
coffee cup or twist—
beads of them in stiff cascades on bottles.

My mother lights one every year
to keep her mother's afterglow unsnuffed.
We sway to them in every kind of darkness.

Their flames are hands protruding
out of leather jacket sleeves,
waving hi when love shows up
and see you when it leaves.

Acknowledgements

Many thanks to Zach Wells, Dan Wells and everyone at Biblioasis; Alexandra Oliver and family; Robyn Sarah, Alex Boyd, Marcus Bales, Kim Bridgford, Claudia Gary, Brian Stanley, James Miller, The Rotary Dial's many fine contributors, Michael Lista, Jason Guriel, and Nathan Whitlock.

Thanks also to Lindsey Love, Heather Power, Tonia Nardi, Rosie Welsh, Haley Wade, Dragana Dosen, Josephine Buettner and Anaya.

Additional thanks to Mariusz Walentynowicz, Andrea Meneghetti, Franco Sgro, Andrew Ferrari, Jiro Shirota and Rachel Piccolotto; to Francesca Avi, Don Augusto and Sanha; to my coworkers old and new, especially Kahn Nomura; to many great customers including Eiko, Michiko, Avalon, Maria, Lauren, Stephanie, and Savanna; and to Centro Trattoria, B'Saha and Alex Rei dos Leitoes.

And lastly thanks to my parents, brothers, aunts, uncles, cousins, sister-in-law, nieces, nephew and friends.

About the Author

Pino Coluccio's first collection, *First Comes Love*, came out in 2005. He has since had work appear in three anthologies and *The Walrus*. He lives in Toronto.